Crystal Victoria

The Vicious Cycle
A Key to Unlocking the Revolving Door

By: Crystal Victoria

Crystal Victoria

The Vicious Cycle: A Key to Unlocking the Revolving Door

© 2014 by Crystal Victoria. All rights reserved.

No part of this book may be reproduced, stored in a retrieval system, or transmitted by any means without the written permission of the author.

ISBN: 9781943240005 (sc)
ISBN: 9781943240012 (ebook)

Library of Congress Control Number: 2012904697

Any people depicted in stock imagery provided by Thinkstock are models, and such images are being used for illustrative purposes only.

Certain stock imagery © Thinkstock.

Because of the dynamic nature of the Internet, any web addresses or links contained in this book may have changed since publication and may no longer be valid. The views expressed in this work are solely those of the author and do not necessarily reflect the views of the publisher, and the publisher hereby disclaims any responsibility for them.

Dedication

To the Creator of the universe from whom all blessings flow. Thank you for blessing us all with divine gifts so that we may serve you and be of service to each other.

To my mother: Thank you for enduring the struggles and loving me anyway in spite of my wayward behavior and mistakes. Without you I wouldn't have made it, and I'm so grateful that you stood the test of faith so that I could be here to write this book for all the families going through this same hardship we've overcome. For all the years you've asked questions, I hope that in this book you find some answers.

To parents and families of loved ones in "The Vicious Cycle": I pray this answers some of your questions about your loved ones and that through this book you see how you can truly help them turn their lives around.

To the people who've been caught in "The Vicious Cycle": In these pages is the way out and the path to a better life. It doesn't hurt to try it, if not for yourself, do it for those who love you. I hope you identify with some of the scenarios and the truth about yourself and this situation.

To the generations of children growing up in our society today: This situation is real life, and my sincere hope for you is that you do not allow this cycle to continue. May this book help you make the right decisions and inspire you to lend a helping hand to those who are lost and struggling in their journey of life.

May we each be inspired to love and be of service to one another as God loves and serves us. It is done.

Crystal Victoria

Table of Contents

Chapter 1: Reality Stinks

Chapter 2: Family Gives Up

Chapter 3: How Do I Survive?

Chapter 4: The Negative Mindset

Chapter 5: The World Kept Spinning

Chapter 6: Readjusting to Freedom

Crystal Victoria

Prologue

    In and out, in and out. Some people just cannot seem to stop the madness. A rare form of insanity; however, it's not so rare. In fact, it's more prevalent than we realize, and its roots reach deeper than most people understand.
    Who on earth wants to be in and out of jail his or her entire life? Isn't once enough?
    Honestly, not for some.
    Why? Well, it's complicated, but the reality is that jail is the easy way out.
    No one really plans it, but after you go a few times it's not all that scary. It's kind of like dying. When you die, you have no worries. Your only fear is the transition or anxiety about how you're going to die. In jail, you don't have too many worries, either. You're just worried about how long you'll be there, and after being in jail a couple of times, the thought of going stops bothering you.
    Worrying in jail will drive you crazy and makes it extra hard to do time. Once you get a grasp of the fact there is nothing you can do, the mind begins to block out most fears of normal life.
    Let's face it—going to jail was probably the biggest fear in the first place. After a few days, you've conquered the fear of the terrible cement place with bars and black and white jumpsuits attached to a ball and chain of which there is no escape. Committing crimes becomes easier once you've conquered that fear. Staying free becomes harder and harder.

Two-thirds of released prisoners are rearrested and one-half are re-incarcerated within three years of release from prison (Langan and Levin, 2002). Rates of recidivism necessarily rise thereafter, so that upwards of 75 percent to 80 percent of released prisoners are likely to be rearrested within a decade of release.

For many men aged 20–40, the prison door is a revolving one. Commit serious crime, get arrested and incarcerated, spend some time in prison, get out, commit more crimes get arrested and incarcerated, and so on. Fifty-six percent of state prisoners released in 1999 had one or more prior convictions, and 25 percent had three or more convictions. Not until men reach their mid-forties does the rate of rearrests fall noticeably.

Is there a cure for this rare form of insanity, which some equate with stupidity? Yes, there is hope. The bad news is that it takes time. My purpose in writing this is to help speed up the process.

The first step to conquering any problem is acknowledging there is one. Know thyself, reader, KNOW THYSELF!

Why should you listen to me, you might ask? Fair enough. So here's how it is. There was a time in my life when I experienced this sort of behavior. In and out, over and over again until I began getting dizzy spinning on that merry-go round. One day I stopped and staggered off, still dizzy from spinning for so long. Like a drunk, I stumbled left and right almost losing my balance a few times trying to regain control of my life. One of the things that kept throwing me off balance was my anger.

I think in some cases the thing that kept me captive in anger was trying to fix things I'd done or make it up to others only to realize that no matter what I did, there was no way of repaying the debts. No amount of money or material things could negate the fact that I'd been absent from someone's life or played a part in someone's misery.

In my first book, *From the Streets to the Skies No Limits,* I wrote about guilt and shame as deadly combinations. Never feel guilty, never feel ashamed. Maybe remorseful, but we all make mistakes and do things we are not proud of. It is all a learning experience, and at some point we must take responsibility for our lives and mistakes, even if those mistakes seemed to be truly out of our control.

This is not to excuse anyone's behavior, but there's no point in committing mental suicide when already being punished physically and restricted to a cell, alone, and away from family and friends.

Enough is enough. Stop it. This same energy spent feeling remorse can be better directed to recreating ourselves and our lives, which can get us out of this mess.

So what exactly is this mess again? It's called "the vicious cycle" and it defines the revolving door of jails, prisons, and institutions. But there is a way out, and it's not easy. It isn't nearly as quick as we might wish it to be, and sometimes some of the mess clings to us for a little while. However, who wants to live in a downward spiral when there is a way out of it?

And there IS a way. Stick with me, and I will show you what it is.

Chapter 1: Reality Stinks

The reality is that all the time spent locked up was wasted. It may have saved a life or two, in which case it was time well spent, but most of the time, for most people, being locked up is a waste of existence. So much can take place in six months to a year or even in a couple of days.

For those locked up, this time is nothing but seconds on a clock. Tick-tock tick-tock tick... playing dominoes, working out, eating, watching TV, writing letters, sleeping, sleeping, sleeping, and sleeping some more.

In some cases people behind bars work or attend classes of some kind. And some people go to church daily, since that's available. They come out of jail or prison with new skills and new beliefs that help them avoid the vicious cycle. For some people, once is enough, but we are **NOT** talking about them.

This book is about the people who make the same mistakes over and over again expecting different results, or to paraphrase Albert Einstein, the insane. Not felon, but insane. We'll talk more about the difference and why I say "insane" later in the book.

Aren't all people frustrated when they find out they have wasted their time? Sometimes we waste time in relationships, a failed business venture, waiting for someone to come by who never shows up. All of these situations are frustrating and so is sitting in jail wasting time only to get out and have the amount of time you wasted smack you in the face.

Sure, if you've lived through this, it's no one's fault but your own, and that makes it hurt even worse. At first when you come home, it is all good. People are glad to see you. You get a breath of fresh air, street

The Vicious Cycle: A Key to Unlocking the Revolving Door

clothes, a good bath, and home-cooked food. It also feels good to have the ability to come and go as you please and even have sex to excess in 24-48 hours.

After that, it all goes downhill and reality sets in. Reality stinks. Deep inside you know you could do better, and it hurts that with all the chances you may have had to either have a better life or start anew, you did not make better choices. For whatever reason, repeatedly you have suffered consequences for bad decision-making. And this reality is a huge disappointment. No one dreams of going to jail and becoming an ex-offender as a kid. Unfortunately, for our youth today, it is cool to be gangster, locked-up, and shot, but has anyone stopped to ask why? Maybe and maybe not, but we're focusing on how to stop the revolving door of jail, a merry-go-round that only lucky ones survive or get off without a scratch. Half of the people making the streets sound cool have never really been in them. They are not about that life. It is called entertainment, not a lifestyle. The ones who do try to live that type of life in the spotlight, end up losing that positive light and some of the money associated with it, too. Lawyers and bond are not cheap; neither are court and probation fees.

The first of the month home is a reality check because you have to remember what it's like to pay bills. A bill? You do not have those in jail, but you do when you are free, along with other responsibilities. In the beginning, everything is fresh and new again. You have made all these promises to yourself and others before release only to break half of them in less than a month. One time I was released after nine months and was back to the same old mess within 24 hours. The reason for this was:

a) I always had an excuse and
b) I got mixed up with that old friend who caught me at that vulnerable "happy to be home" weak state of mind.

Yes, I could have made wiser choices, like working out and hanging out with someone else. But I didn't, and for that reason I was responsible for the mistakes I made. So is everyone else. It is always best to find the part you played in the situation regardless of whether it is truly your fault. The only way to move forward and make wiser decisions is by accepting responsibility for everything that happens to you. No one likes to admit making mistakes, but it is crucial to the growth process.

How old you are and how much time you have when you first are locked up affects how frustrated you will be when you come home. The longer and older, or longer and younger, the worse it is.

Keyword—*longer*, as in length of time you have to sit locked up. Birthdays and holidays all become another day, and on top of that you're spending these significant days with people you don't really know. How odd is that?

If reality is frustrating enough and you previously had a drug problem, chances are you will have a worse one when you come home because you just cannot deal. It is too much to just accept the reality that you have made jail a revolving door. Why wasn't once enough? What is wrong with you? This is a topic for a whole other book, which we will not get into in this one. Substance abuse is also a reason some make jail a revolving door. As all great specialists in this area say, "Drugs are a symptom of a much larger problem."

In this case, jail as a revolving door is the problem, and the fact that our lives are not what we want them to be does not help us stay sober. Sometimes we give up on ourselves, and that's either before or after the family gives up, which leads us to the next chapter.

Chapter 2: Family Gives Up

Those wonderful people with whom we share blood can also be the biggest setback in our reintegration into society. Sometimes they cannot help themselves because they don't know any better. They do not know how to handle or respond to our actions.

We teach others how to treat us. If we are treating ourselves badly, how can we get mad when other people treat us the same way? After a while, they get sick of helping and we get sick of asking or needing it. We are disappointed in ourselves and feel guilty, ashamed, or both. We only want our loved ones to know we are sorry, but it is not the easiest thing to do when you just come home. It takes time to find ourselves and figure out what to do next. It is a process that requires strength and determination, and our society does not make it any easier. In some cases, people use all these reasons to correct their behavior as the very excuses they continue to do wrong.

Can you imagine what it is like to have a parent, spouse, or child die while you are in jail and you cannot get to them, the funeral, or the people in your family for support? I experienced this, and it was truly the turning point. After my grandfather passed while I was incarcerated, I was truly done. My greatest fear had been my mother or grandmother dying, but my grandfather was just as bad. We expected it to happen, but the reality of it was a different story.

Gratefully, I was able to get a one-day release on two occasions to go see him, but while I was locked up, all I thought about was how much time I could've spent with him if I wouldn't have been getting into all kinds of unnecessary mess. All that time I was incarcerated could have been spent with my grandfather, but we take our loved ones for granted as if they will be here forever. They will not be here forever, and you never know when it will be their time or yours. Time is a valuable resource because it is the only thing you cannot get back once it is wasted or gone.

Children. You leave when they are babies and decide to straighten up when they are a teen. Try to act like a parent then. See how that works. If they are extremely frustrated with your absence, they will treat you like a stranger. There is no way to know which way the pendulum will swing. It's a roll of the dice. Most children are forgiving, but our own guilt about our absence from their lives drives us to want to take care of everything to make it up. You cannot always do so. You have to let go and learn to accept that you missed it. You missed their first words, first step, first bicycle ride, first day of school, and who knows how many birthdays. You cannot get that time and those moments back.

Seeing you behind the glass or at visitation does not mean you were in their lives. That means someone loved you enough to make sure your kids made it to see you or at least sent you letters and pictures. Therein lies another reason to feel guilty.

To have a good spouse or mate at home is a blessing. Especially when they stay with you, take care of you and the kids, and make sure you handle business when you come home. Everyone is not so lucky. Most of the time, your spouse or mate leaves, and you have to let him or her go because for you to beg them to stay would be selfish. Why should he or she give up his or her life or time for a mistake you made? Why should someone suffer every day missing and thinking about you when you did not care enough to stay out of trouble?

On the flip side, why did someone choose you knowing you were caught in the vicious cycle? Nevertheless, that is another topic, let's stick to the script.

It's a given that your loved one was probably with someone else since you were gone, but you don't care because you were locked up. Why should you be upset unless you are completely selfish? It is the thought of that person you love with someone else, and the fact that they were well within their rights that will hurt you.

Some of our parents did the same thing we did. In and out, in and out. The vicious cycle is sometimes a generational curse. At some point, it must be broken, and it starts with you. However, if your parents were not a partaker in this lifestyle, then they truly will never understand you. Another purpose of this book.

The people responsible for bringing us into this world suffer the most for our actions. We think we are only hurting ourselves, but our families do suffer with us. We think they don't care, but they do in their own way. They also have their own way of showing it, and sometimes it is called tough love.

Of course, they are happy when we get released, but understand they fear us coming home and going back to jail again, especially if we have done so before. We tell them things about how we are going to change and after we make mistakes again, they feel just as silly for believing us as we do for making promises.

The guilt, the shame is deadly and leads to more mistakes. Those who do not go into a "fuck it" way of thinking after this are strong, very strong. Sometimes parents do not know we are just as disappointed in ourselves as they are in us, but it is hard to put into words. To them, it is logical, "Just stop it already!"

To us, it is not so simple, and like any learned behavior or habit, it takes time to break. We did not get into that mindset overnight, and it will not cure overnight.

For the parents reading this, know that the key is to love your sons and daughters anyway. Never give up. That is easier said than done; especially when repeatedly you have done all you can to help. Just keep on supporting your son or daughter no matter what. They really mean it when they say they are not going to repeat their mistakes. It just might not happen as fast as either you or they would like it to.

And parents, don't let feelings of guilt complicate matters. It is truly not your fault, and your guilt will get in the way of truly supporting efforts to change.

Chapter 3: How Do I Survive?

Legally, of course!

Wait, you may not remember what that means. It means to do something legit to make money and take care of yourself. For example, working a job, starting a business, or going to school. It means being a responsible adult.

So what happens when you have never done any of the above? Start today and make a decision to do something differently, and then try it.

Jobs for those who have served time, if you find one, usually pay very low. It may require long hours or two jobs to make ends meet. How do you work long hours or two jobs while on probation/parole reporting, taking classes, and doing community service too?

Parole/probation officers want to keep you busy so you will stay out of trouble, but the truth is they put way more on you than the average person can stand. Yes, some do make it and it is those success stories that justify the continuance of harsh demands better known as "probation/parole conditions".

The solution is this: Do what you have to do to get out of the system and once you do, DO NOT get back into the vicious cycle. How to get and stay out will be discussed later in the book.

How do you live? Or better yet, where do you live?

Honestly, very few apartments accept people who have served time. Pretty crazy, huh? They have their reasons and they are valid, but there are other options like transitional housing and shelters, which are available in your area. Check with your local courthouse and community centers.

Privately owned houses, condos, or townhomes for rent are good options also. By talking to the owner and explaining the situation in person, face to face, they may be willing to give you a chance. Once you get that chance, do not mess up your living arrangement by making that person sorry he or she helped you. All this does is make it harder for those who truly do need a chance and are willing to change. It's also not fair to the person who is giving you a chance.

If you feel like you are going to mess up again, care enough to talk to the property owner about your difficulties and move out. By talking to them, you're establishing a relationship built on trust. They may just let you stay, but by giving them the ability to choose, you won't burn a bridge or destroy a chance someone else may need.

In some cases, someone goes to jail extremely wealthy from the events that landed them there. Meaning big drug dealers, white-collar criminals, and other scam artists. They are everywhere and in every industry. If this were not the case *American Greed* would not be a show. If you never seen it, watch one or two episodes and you will see what I mean. These people have the hardest time changing their behavior. Why? Because it pays and pays big! Trust me, if you were in their position, it would be hard for you to stop, too.

However, like with all criminal activity, no matter how well it pays, it has an expiration date. You never know when that is. It is better to get out when you can, as fast as you can. When you come home, you will have an "x" on your back like everybody else who has been locked up. No one is an exception to the rules. Forget expunging and sealing. Repeat offenders will permanently be marked, and your reputation gets worse with each offense.

In some cases people are caught up in the same behavior because no job will pay them even close to what they were making doing things their own way. This does not justify the behavior, and I am not encouraging anyone to repeat the behavior just because I can understand how tempting it is to return to the lifestyle that had money rolling in. I am just recognizing that reality because it is important to address all crimes large and small. By doing so, this book leaves no stone unturned or people serving time omitted.

People who illegally make millions of dollars a year are the best at what they do, and when they are making that kind of money, they have been doing it a long time. That is an old habit that dies hard. If they come home and go back, don't be surprised. It is more than a criminal mentality, they are downright spoiled, and their ego will not let them even consider $7.50 per hour.

The solution is to start somewhere, even if it is small. In everything, look for solutions and take the opportunities that come your way. They may lead to bigger and better ones down the road. By taking steps and working hard, you have a chance for a promotion or a raise to increase your earning potential. It may not happen quickly or overnight, but overtime it is more rewarding. And the best thing? It's legal!

Even if there aren't opportunities to advance in that particular job, by showing you're a good employee, when you apply for another job someplace else, you'll have a good reference that will prove not only CAN you change, but that you HAVE changed. It will open up doors for you. Stick with this, and you WILL get better jobs. Particularly if you are also taking classes to improve your skills.

Survival is difficult, but it can be done as long as you stop making excuses and start taking action. Patience is a virtue, and self-control will take you farther than you may expect.

Like I said earlier, it took time to get where you were in your bad choices, so it is going to take some time to turn that all around. But do the right thing, be patient, and you will break the vicious cycle.

If you are trying to help someone who has made mistakes, you need to be patient here, too, and maybe offer some help. For example, offer $1 an hour for every hour they go to work. That is only $40 a week out of your pocket, but it shows your son, daughter, boyfriend, girlfriend, granddaughter, grandson, or whatever that you believe in them and are there to help.

Chapter 4: The Negative Mindset

The negative mindset will keep you trapped in the vicious cycle every time. This mindset will help you turn your motivations into excuses to do wrong. A lot of these are boldface lies we tell ourselves to excuse our behavior and take an easy way out. That easy way will keep you in the vicious cycle.

Some of the lies include:

"I'm a bad person."

"I'm a criminal."

"I've already been once, so I may as well go ahead and keep doing what I've been doing."

"It's not that bad and neither is jail."

"They can't keep me forever, I'll get out."

"I'm trying to make this money, so I gotta do what I gotta do."

"My family needs to eat."

"I gotta eat. Eat greedy."

"I have to get back on my feet."

"I'm a deadbeat dad or mom."

"No one helped me, why should I care?"

"I'm only hurting myself."

"It's not my fault, if it wasn't for _____, I wouldn't be here."

"I knew I shouldn't done that, I should've waited another day then I wouldn't have got caught."

"I shouldn't have made that left/right and got pulled over."

"Fuck the police and my P.O."

"My dad/mom has been in and out my whole life, so I was destined to be here, too."

"I can't read or write, so I gotta hustle."

"I make too much money to quit."

"This is easier than being free. I ain't gotta pay no bills and get three hots and a cot (three meals a day and a bed)."

"My mom/dad left me and I had to raise myself in these streets."

"I'm a gangsta/thug living that gangsta/thug life."

"I pay the cost to be the boss."

"I'm gonna hustle til I die."

"I ain't gonna change. This is me."

"The devil made me do it. Satan was in my way."

"I do what I wanna do."

"Fuck the world, ain't nobody ever gave a damn about me."

"No one gives me anything, so what else you expect me to do?"

"This is the downfall of black men. White people want us in jail."

"They locked me up for no reason."

"The world owes me a living, I did this or I did that."

"I just smoke weed/crack on weekends."

"It was only a molly and some pills."

"All I had was an ounce that ain't shit. So and so had three kilos and got less time than me. It's not fair."

"No one loves me, and I have no family."

"This is all I know. I don't know how to do anything else."

"I'm good at this. I'm doing what I'm good at."

"I took from a business that was already stealing from people so that's what they get. It's a tax deduction. They'll get it back at the beginning of the year."

"I've made so many mistakes; I'll never amount to anything."

And the list goes on and on and on. The ugly truth. This is what repeat offenders tell themselves as an excuse for bad behavior and decision making. You probably have some creative excuses yourself, but the ones above are the ones most commonly used. Now some of these things are valid reasons to be frustrated with life and other people. However, you do not have to be a victim of that frustration. If you are frustrated, get help, talk to somebody, and get some kind of counseling.

Your PO will be able to give you resources to get free counseling. You can also go online and see what your county has to offer. There are community groups set up to help you. They will have resources for low-cost or even free counseling. Even if you're not religious, you can go to a church and ask them for community resources. You can also call a local college and ask them if they have free counseling through a Master's degree in social work program. A lot of times, students working on advanced degrees have to do free counseling under a trained professional as part of getting a degree. Both the YMCA and YWCA also often have counseling available, and if they don't, they will know all about the free services offered in your area. And counseling is confidential. Unless you are going to hurt yourself or somebody else, counselors cannot talk to anybody about anything you tell them.

Going in and out of jail is not the answer, nor is it helping you any, so stop it. Some of the excuses I listed at the beginning of this chapter should be motivation to change and do better.

If you have problems reading and writing, you can find free literacy classes in your community. One of the best things you can ever do for yourself is to learn to read and write.

If you see yourself as a deadbeat mom or dad, take some parenting classes and make an effort to connect with your kids. This isn't only good for you, but it will help your kids, too. Most kids want to look up to their parents, to know their parents are there for them, and in return, they give a lot of love and support.

If your mom and dad left you to survive on the streets, then prove to yourself that you can survive legitimately. You are strong enough, tough enough, smart enough, and resourceful enough that you do not have to live the way they did. You can get it right, no matter how bad their example was.

It is my belief that in some cases the enemy is the "inner-me." The devil is not always necessarily outside of you or me. It is within us, just as God is within us. There is spiritual warfare going on within ourselves and within our world, which takes away our inner peace. People do not always understand the depth of this fact. We are spiritual beings having a human experience. Therefore, our spiritual side (which is God, our spirit) wars with our human side (which is flesh, ego, "devil", enemy). When we learn to cleanse our minds with positive thoughts, we will begin to master our lives and our actions. It starts with the mind. Whatever ideas and thoughts you hold in your mind, may manifest or be attracted to you. Mind controls man.

If you take responsibility for what you feel the devil is doing to your life, I promise you will take away its power. By always blaming an outside entity or spirit for your actions or other things all of the time, you will never accept responsibility for changing it.

Everyone we meet or come into contact with is a reflection of ourselves: the good, the bad, and the ugly. So next time someone irritates the hell out of you, remember you have irritated a few people in your life as well; therefore, they are just like you in a sense. To expand on that, sometimes you are getting what you have given to somebody else. In my book *From the Streets to the Skies No Limits: Diary of a Boss Lady,* I began to explain what karma really is all about and how this is spiritual law, not just a cliché or a trendy term. It is a fact of life:

> "There is a reason the Bible says, 'Do unto others as you would have them do unto you,' 'Whatever you sow, you shall reap,' 'Do not grow weary in well doing, for in due time you shall reap, ' 'Turn the other cheek, ' and 'Vengeance is mine saith the Lord.'

The Vicious Cycle: A Key to Unlocking the Revolving Door

> *"These verses (as well as others) point to one spiritual law: karma. The law of cause and effect. Like a boomerang, the law of karma creates balance and harmony. The law works to ensure life balances.. All good actions are rewarded or given a karmic benefit and the "not-so-good actions" will result in "not-so-good" consequences. This does not mean punishment, but it is what must happen to restore a balance. Without karma, there is no peace, harmony, or balance. The reason for this is because no one will learn understanding and compassion until each knows how it feels to be on both sides of the coin."*
>
> –Crystal Victoria, From the Streets to the Skies No Limits

There are other spiritual laws besides the law of karma, but this is not the book for that, nor am I messenger for those lessons. Pay attention and life will show you all you need to know. In due time, you will have that "aha" moment when the light bulb above your head comes on and your spiritual eyes are opened. Before I leave the topic of spiritual law, allow me to give you one last demonstration on how they definitely work.

Take gravity for example. If you jump off a building without a parachute, machine, or into some water, you will hit the ground. It will happen like this every time. Whether you're a good person, bad person, religious, or even if you prayed and asked God to make you fly before you jump, you're still going down. By the grace of God, you may not die when you hit the ground, but you're going down, and you will land somewhere. You do not have to believe in gravity for it to exist or work.

The same goes for karma and other spiritual laws. You never have to believe or accept any of them, but that does not keep them from affecting your life. We live in harmony with gravity by not jumping off buildings without protection or some other kind of cushion. We should also live in harmony with the other laws.

If we live in harmony with the law of karma, then we will always treat others the way we wish to be treated, sow good things, think good thoughts, and not seek revenge. If instead we treat others badly, do bad things, think bad thoughts, and seek revenge, life will balance out and the seeds we have sown may hurt us. God sees everything, and we never get away with anything, not even our thoughts.

It is only a matter of time before our thoughts and actions either help or harm us. Choose wisely. Look at your life, and think of all the times you have done something that has come back to you, good or bad. You will see exactly what I am talking about. You will have all the proof you need. Now what do you want? Good karma or bad? To break that vicious cycle or to be trapped in it and the misery that comes with it forever?

Chapter 5: The World Kept Spinning

What do I mean when I say the world kept spinning? Simple. You have been gone so long, in and out of your little world, that you missed technology advancements. What is LinkedIn? What is an app? How are you supposed to fill out job applications online?

Some of these things have everyone puzzled. You are not alone, but you are definitely behind. Don't have an email? You are a dinosaur, sorry. If you do not catch up, you are ability to thrive and have a life will be extinct.

In some jails and prisons, you can take computer classes and things of that nature. Let's say you took some classes and learned how to apply for jobs online. Like all skills, if you don't use it, you will lose it. You must practice that which you want to do and do well.

You must also be open to learning and unlearning things. This takes patience, self-control, and time. Sometimes we get frustrated trying to learn something new. Everyone does, but keep trying. Persistence is the difference between successful and unsuccessful people. Successful people never quit or give up; they keep trying over and over again in a positive way.

This quote by Calvin Coolidge is one of my favorite ways to look at persistence. When I was starting a new business that had me scared, a man came along and implanted this in my brain. That was a couple of years ago, and I am grateful to that man because I have been successful after memorizing this quote.

> *"Nothing in the world takes the place of persistence. Talent will not; nothing is more common than unsuccessful men with talent. Genius will not; unrewarded genius is almost a proverb. Education will not; the world is full of educated derelicts. Persistence and determination alone are omnipotent. The slogan 'Press on' has solved and always will solve the problems of the human race."* –Calvin Coolidge, 30th U.S. President

Now after reading this, you are probably asking what is a derelict? After a great quote like that, all you noticed was the one word you do not understand? A derelict is a bum, beggar, castaway, outcast, hobo... you get the picture. Honestly, I had to look the word up, too. Now that you know what the word means, read the quote again and again until you totally understand that trying over and over and over is what you need to do to succeed.

Another thing that makes you feel a little out of date when you first are released is that the places you once went to are not the same. Maybe they have been remodeled into something else, torn down, or no one goes there anymore, leaving you with the long, drawn-out task of finding something else to do or making some changes.

Change equals money. You believe me, don't you? Add up some change in your pocket and I promise you have some money. It may not be much, but it's something. At the same time, making a change in your life will equal some money, if you make enough of the right positive ones.

Making changes usually goes hand in hand with the people you associate yourself with. You are going to have friends doing better than you and some doing the same things they were doing when you left.

Which friends do you choose? It makes a difference. Friends that are doing better than you are and have made some changes themselves will encourage you. Do not let the fact they are doing better intimidate you to the point of choosing to hang around the other group.

The friends doing the same things will have you doing the same things before you know it. They may not directly encourage you, but being around them is part of the vicious cycle that makes it easier for you to be sucked back in to that lifestyle. Yeah, I know, they're probably more fun than the other is, but how much fun is that vicious cycle? None, right?

Sticking with the friends doing better than you should encourage you to reach their level, not inspire you to pull them down or make you jealous. There is nothing to be jealous of. I read somewhere that people who are jealous of others are only jealous of a struggle wrapped in strength. If you really knew and understood other people's struggles, you may find that you are glad you do not have them. At some point, you could have made decisions to get you where they are, but you did not, so do not punish them for it. It is not your friend's fault you made bad decisions.

When people choose to become successful, the first thing they are hit with is, "Man you changed. You are different." Well, yeah, they did change. So what? You probably need to make some changes instead of being worried about theirs.

It is not even really that they have changed. What happens is when you decide to pursue a goal or a purpose; you must allow the journey to make your mind strong to achieve it. They have not changed; they just make wiser decisions because they are on a mission. If you make a decision to pursue a mission or goal, you will become wiser, also.

If you have tunnel vision when it comes to accomplishing something, everything that does not aid in your quest tends to fall away, including habits, behaviors, and people (family included).

It is called sacrifice. You make sacrifices in life to get what you want and become all that you are meant to be. Napoleon Hill states in his book *Laws of Success,* "Successful people find a way to get what they want and have what they want WITHOUT violating the rights of others."

We all have the ability to be great. It starts with and takes a firm decision to do so and then to take action on your decision. Don't just sit around and talk about it, be about it. Do it. If you do not know where to start, start by building the confidence necessary to ask for help. Read books, start going to different places, and hanging around new people who can teach you something.

Do not be afraid to be honest with yourself and others. Not everyone is going to accept, understand, or like you. Some people will be afraid to trust you. It's okay—understand that if circumstances were reversed, you would feel the same way. Get over it and keep making positive changes.

Chapter 6: Readjusting to Freedom

We all are fully aware that nowadays it is difficult to reintegrate into society with an "x" on your back. No one said it would be easy, but I will tell you it is worth it. You know the old clichés, what doesn't kill you makes you stronger, and nothing worth having comes easy. Well, they are true.

That said, I will agree with you and state that it should not be as hard as it is, but at this point, we have to live with it.

Now for one moment I am going to highlight how unfair you are going to have it. In fact, I am going to actually agree. I'm not excusing the fact that you must work hard if you want to get your life right, nor am I justifying your stay in the "vicious cycle".

In case you do not know what people are calling you when they say "felon", we are going to talk about it. If you notice I have not used that term in this book, I use "ex-offender". Even that term irritates me, but here is what society thinks of you now and this is what you must overcome.

Why don't I like the label "felon?" We may be many things, but a felon has a very negative meaning behind it and who said that it was okay to use the term? Or convicts for the convicted? Who was the first to cast this stone for it to ricochet and knock everyone out? Or did someone go to jail and call himself or herself a convicted felon and when they got out, everybody thought it was a good name? I wanted an answer, so I did some research and this is what I found on Dictionary.com:

> "Felon, c.1300, from O.Fr. felon "evil-doer, scoundrel, traitor, rebel, the Devil," from M.L. fellonem "evil-doer," of uncertain origin, perhaps from Frank. *fillo, *filljo "person who whips or beats, scourger" (cf. O.H.G. fillen "to whip"); or from L. fel "gall, poison," on the notion of "one full of bitterness."
>
> Another theory (advanced by Professor R. Atkinson of Dublin) traces it to L. fellare "to suck" (see fecund), which had an obscene secondary meaning in classical Latin (well-known to readers of Martial and Catullus), which would make a felon, etymologically, a "cock-sucker." The Oxford English Dictionary inclines toward the "gall" explanation, but finds Atkinson's the "most plausible" of the others"

To get the definition straight, a felon is nothing but a cock-sucker and evildoer. The definition of this word is truly heartbreaking to know it describes people. Felon also means *purulent inflammation of the end joint of a finger, sometimes affecting the bone or an acute and painful inflammation of the deeper tissues of a finger or toe, usually near the nail.* To sum it up nicely, it means a royal pain, menace, or an irritation.

In a recent article Margaret Colgate Love, who formerly served as a U.S. Pardon Attorney in the 1990s, offers her viewpoint and historical information on the word "felon".

> *"Felon" is an ugly label that confirms the debased status that accompanies conviction. It identifies a person as belonging to a class outside many protections of the law, someone who can be freely discriminated against, someone who exists at the margins of society.*
>
> *In short, a "felon" is a legal outlaw and social outcast.*
> *The word "felon" conjures up images of large, scary people (men, of course) whose goal in life is to steal my things and hurt me. Affixing an "ex-" changes nothing. Felons deserve a wide berth and whatever opprobrium they get.*

The Vicious Cycle: A Key to Unlocking the Revolving Door

> *And yet that is the label they must bear, in the workplace, in their communities, and in society at large. It is an unhelpful label and in many cases it is deeply unfair.*
>
> *In the Middle Ages, and even in the early days of our own Republic, felony convictions were hanging affairs, and civil death statutes simply anticipated the impending corporal end. After the Civil War, felonies expanded to include many minor property crimes (Mississippi's infamous "pig law" is illustrative), and prosecution became a convenient way of disenfranchising and re-enslaving the recently-freed black population.*
>
> *…These days, you don't have to do anything particularly evil to be condemned to what sentencing scholar Nora Demleitner has called "internal exile." The "felon" label now applies to more than 20 million Americans.*
>
> *However, labeling people as "felons" is also fundamentally at war with efforts to reduce the number of people in prison, to facilitate reentry, and to encourage those who have committed a crime, or even many crimes, to become law-abiding and productive citizens.*
>
> *The word "felon" (and for that matter other less ugly but still degrading labels like "offender," with or without the feckless prefix "ex-") is no less dysfunctional. We can do better.""*

*site source- http://www.thecrimereport.org/viewpoints/2012-03-whats-in-a-name-a-lot-when-the-name-is-felon

Instead of labeling people as felons, there should be first, second, and third degree insanity cases. Why? Because to be in the vicious cycle means making the same mistakes over and over again expecting different results, or to paraphrase Albert Einstein, insanity. Not felon, but insane.

Who created the word felon for insane people, and why didn't they just call it what it was, insanity? No wonder some people rebel when they get out with that label attached to them. Are people in jail with a felony actually felons? No.

Let this be another lesson about why you have to get out of the system and get your life on track. For some reason, people have a right to

35

call you this and if you get mad, you are out of line. If I am called a felon or anything else, that is first-degree insanity in my book. Now we both could potentially be in a position to act like felons. I have honestly seen some people walk on temporary insanity for some crap that was seriously felon as hell, and I know for a fact you have, too.

Of course being called a felon is unfair. You have done time and been away from family. When you go home, it is going to be tougher finding a job and almost impossible to find a decent place to live in your own name. People are going to stereotype you and call you a "felon" and other names that you may not deserve.

You are going to get so frustrated and irritated with life enough that you might not even want to get out of bed in the morning, and when you do get up, you might detest everything and everybody you see. That is normal, we all feel that way some days, but do not stay there stuck in that mentality. Develop a healthy routine for positive living and thinking. Personally, I use meditation.

What is meditation? Why is it important to meditate? What do you meditate on? Is meditation reserved for a specific religious denomination? Is meditation against Christianity or any other belief system? How do you meditate? I am glad you asked.

First, I will explain what meditation is and why it is important to meditate. An ordinary person may consider meditation as a worship or prayer. But it is not so. Meditation has one goal and it is to slow down and, eventually, completely stop the continuous activity of our minds. It is a state of profound, deep peace that occurs when the mind is calm and silent, yet completely alert. It is normally very difficult to stop our minds all together, so it does take lots of practice. In reality, meditation is a state of thoughtless awareness.

One great reason to meditate is that meditation is considered by a number of researchers as potentially one of the most effective forms of stress reduction and has the potential to improve quality of life and decrease healthcare costs. Meditation is effortless and leads to a state of 'thoughtless awareness' in which the excessive stress producing activity of the mind is neutralized without reducing alertness and effectiveness.

The Vicious Cycle: A Key to Unlocking the Revolving Door

Authentic meditation enables one to focus on the present moment rather than dwell on the unchangeable past or undetermined future.

Sources of information:
Hassed C. Meditation in general practice. Aust Fam Physician 1996; 25(8):1257–1260.

West M (ed). The psychology of meditation. Oxford: Clarendon Press, 1987.

Achterberg J. Mind body interventions, meditation. In: Berman B. Alternative medicine, expanding medical horizons. Washington DC: Office of Alternative Medicine, National Institute of Health, 1992.

Even the Bible has verses, which encourage meditation as a general practice, like it does prayer. Genesis 24:63 (KJV) "And Isaac went out to meditate in the field at the eventide: and he lifted up his eyes, and saw, and, behold, the camels were coming." Joshua 1:8 (KJV) "This book of the law shall not depart out of thy mouth; but thou shalt meditate therein day and night, that thou mayest observe to do according to all that is written therein: for then thou shalt make thy way prosperous, and then thou shalt have good success." Psalms 77:12 (KJV) "I will meditate also of all thy work, and talk of thy doings." 1 Timothy 4:15 (KJV) "Meditate upon these things; give thyself wholly to them; that thy profiting may appear to all."

Every morning and every night, I meditate using a few simple techniques. These techniques are borrowed from the Rosicrucians (www.amorc.org), and can be used by anyone at anytime of the day or night. Who and what is a Rosicrucian? The short answer is one who studies spiritual and natural laws, in order to live in harmony with them and achieve self-mastery. If you want more information, I suggest you find out for yourself.

Steps:
1. Sit in a chair or other comfortable place with your back straight, feet flat on the floor, and your hands on your thighs palms down.
2. Close your eyes.
3. Inhale and exhale deeply through the nose ONLY for a few minutes.
4. Listen to your breathing and feel your body relax.
5. Visualize earth as seen from space.

6. Send positive thoughts toward the planet earth. Use words like healing, peace, love, community, forgiveness, harmony, appreciation, support, motivation, wisdom, understanding, joy, etc.

7. Now picture a person you know who needs prayer or assistance.
8. Visualize the person in front of you and see them as happy, healthy, calm, and at peace.
9. Now visualize yourself and picture yourself being successful, at peace, healed, and joyful.
10. After doing this for about 10 minutes, stop and say, "Thank you, God. It is done."

Another technique that works extremely well is doing the same basic technique but saying "God" mentally or in a low voice every time you inhale and exhale for about five minutes a day. The steps are listed below:

1. Sit in a chair or other comfortable place with your back straight, feet flat on the floor, and your hands on your thighs palms down.
2. Close your eyes.
3. Inhale deeply through the nose and say "God," and exhale deeply through the nose and say "God."
4. Repeat for about five minutes or fifty times.

Now we come to understanding how we repay the debts. Understand you are going to have to repay the debts, and I do not mean physically or on your own power in every case. Life is going to give you the real lesson. Ever notice how it seems like as soon as you start trying to do better and get your life on track, everything you could possibly imagine goes wrong? It is not all in your head. That is exactly what is happening to you. You are repaying the debts at that moment.

Everything that comes along and knocks you down, and attempts to stop you from moving forward is only life balancing out your previous behavior. It has to happen for you to move forward.

The Vicious Cycle: A Key to Unlocking the Revolving Door

Do not stop, KEEP GOING! It does not get easier, but you get much stronger. When you seem to be getting attacked the hardest, do all you can to keep moving and working through it. If you want better out of life, you are going to have to break through the barriers.

Maybe it has come to stop you, but I will not tell you it is the devil. Sometimes, it's life's way of making us stronger and helping us get rid of and purge our flaws and imperfections. In some cases, it is life's way of taking everything wrong you have done to yourself and other people and giving it to you all at once or when you least expect it.

Suck it up and take it, just as you gave it out. This too shall pass and when the storm is over, you are going to be on the other side smelling like a rose and a lot stronger than you were prior to the storm. The good part about your strength is it will help you make wiser decisions when every temptation to do wrong comes your way.

For example, you may not have much money in your pocket for long periods of time. You see some old friends still selling and you're tempted to hit the streets. You want to go grab some drugs (or whatever you sell) and go on a super selling spree because you know you have it in you.

What do you do if you do not want to end up back in jail?

This is where the strength you have built from battling to do right comes in. It will not let you go back to your old ways. You have worked too damn hard to get your life straight to even risk one minor mess up. You are too close to a good life, and you do not want to get caught back in the vicious cycle. Your mind has become so strong that everything in you doesn't just say, "No" it shouts, "HELL, NO!!"

This is a test and you must pass. This is a fight for your life! The police could be sitting waiting on you on the next block to mess up. Maybe they are not there today, but they will be there tomorrow. In their minds they are saying, "I knew he/she wasn't strong enough. I knew we would get to lock him/her back up. Ha-ha what a loser! He/she'll never stay out of jail."

Do not prove them right. Prove yourself right! You must make the right decision or else you will face all of the obstacles that you just made it through all over again from the beginning. This is the transition you must go through to make it through the other side. You can do it.

Remember these:

"Just this once or one last time."

"I've already been once, so I may as well go ahead and keep doing what I've been doing."

"It's not that bad and neither is jail."

"They can't keep me forever, I'll get out."

"I'm trying to make this money, so I gotta do what I gotta do."

"My family needs to eat."

"I gotta eat. Eat greedy."

"I have to get back on my feet."

"I knew I shouldn't have done that, I should've waited another day then I wouldn't have got caught."

"I shouldn't have made that left/right and got pulled over."

"Fuck the police and my P.O."

"I'm only hurting myself."

"This is all I know. I don't know how to do anything else."

"I'm good at this. I'm doing what I'm good at."

"I won't get caught if I only do it this once or this week."

THESE ARE LIES. You are lying to yourself. The devil in you is lying to you.

You know it, but will what you now know from reading this book empower you to do better? It will if you  accept that this lifestyle has an expiration date. How do you want to expire... death or jail? You never know how you will die, nor do you have a choice. However, you do have a choice how to live your life.

The Vicious Cycle: A Key to Unlocking the Revolving Door

Some people will go ahead and keep on messing up. Go ahead. Keep going until you get tired. Keep going until your family disowns you completely and your kids forget who you are. Keep going until you really don't have another choice, and you drift through life merely existing instead of living to your full potential. Keep going and looking over your shoulder worried about your next move being your last. Keep going until you are locked up when your parents or loved ones are on their sick bed about to die, and you can't tell them you love them one last time. By all means, keep going if this is how you want this to end.

What do you do when you're not done, and when you get out you're going right back to the same old thing? Keep going till you get tired and this book will still be here to guide you out again. Make sure you pick it up and take notes next time. I do not oppose anyone to learning the hard way, and I will not deprive you of the experience.

There are plenty of resources for those who want better. Check your cities local workforce centers and nonprofit organizations. I guarantee you there is help and there is hope. There is a solution for all of your excuses and someone there ready to help. Don't be afraid to ask and be completely honest with others and, even more importantly, first be honest with yourself. Admit that you either like jail or are just used to it and don't know any better. Whichever one it is, once you acknowledge the problem so you can change.

The following story is a very important one. My hope is that it inspires you.

Are you a Carrot an Egg or a Coffee Bean?

A young woman went to her grandmother and told her about her life and how things were so hard for her. She did not know how she was going to make it and wanted to give up. She was tired of fighting and struggling. It seemed that as soon as one problem was solved, a new one arose.

Her grandmother took her to the kitchen. She filled three pots with water and placed each on a high fire. Soon the pots came to a boil. In the *first, she placed carrots, in the second she placed eggs, and the last she placed ground coffee beans. She let them sit and boil, without saying a word.*

In about twenty minutes she turned off the burners. She fished the carrots out and placed them in a bowl. She then pulled the eggs out and placed them in a bowl. Then she ladled the coffee out and placed it in a bowl.
Turning to her granddaughter, she asked, "Tell me, what do you see?"
"Carrots, eggs, and coffee," she replied.

She brought her closer and asked her to feel the carrots. She did and noted that they were soft. She then asked her to take an egg and break it. After pulling off the shell, she observed the hard-boiled egg. Finally, she asked her to sip the coffee. The daughter smiled as she tasted its rich aroma.

The granddaughter then asked, "What does it mean, Grandmother?"

Her grandmother explained that each of these objects had faced the same adversity — boiling water — but each reacted differently. The carrot went in strong, hard and unrelenting. However, after being subjected to the boiling water, it softened and became weak. The egg had been fragile. Its thin outer shell had protected its liquid interior. But, after sitting through the boiling water, its inside became hardened. The ground coffee beans were unique, however. After they were in the boiling water, they had changed the water.

"Which are you?" she asked her granddaughter. "When adversity knocks on your door, how do you respond? Are you a carrot, an egg, or a coffee bean?"

Think of this: Which am I? Am I the carrot that seems strong, but with pain and adversity I wilt and become soft and lose my strength? Am I the egg that starts with a malleable heart, but changes with the heat? Did I have a fluid spirit, but after a death, a breakup, a financial hardship or some other trial, have I become hardened and stiff? Does my shell look the same, but on the inside am I bitter and tough with a stiff spirit and a hardened heart?

Or am I like the coffee bean? The bean actually changes the hot water, the very circumstance that brings the pain. When the water gets hot, it releases the fragrance and flavor of your life. If you are like the bean, when things are at their worst, you get better and change the situation around you. When the hours are the darkest and trials are their greatest, do you elevate to another level?
How do you handle adversity? Are you changed by your surroundings or do you bring life, flavor, to them?

ARE YOU A CARROT, AN EGG, OR A COFFEE BEAN?

Do you wander how you can become a coffee bean? How about a coffee maker? (Haha, seriously though.) A coffee maker is someone who can hold a group of coffee beans while being subjected to hot water and make a whole pot of coffee.

Let me break it down. You start as a coffee bean changing your own circumstances to the point where other people notice. They want your help. They want to know how you do it. You say sure and you bring them on board. When the boiling hot water (also known as "life") starts hitting them and they want to give up, it's you who says, "Just hang in there. I got you."

And you provide strength through their storms. Sooner or later you'll have many people you've helped and who need your help going through storms. Because you're there to help, you'll feel some of it, too, but you'll be strong enough to help them overcome adversity. Over and over again this happens until every coffee bean has made a small serving of coffee in a huge coffee pot. There you are: you have your pot of coffee and you are now a coffee maker.

To become a coffee bean is really a three-step process which I worked one step at a time very slowly. The first step is change the way you think. The second step is control your emotions. The third step is finding a new method of stress relief or something you love to do. It's that simple but it's not easy.

Step 1- Change the Way You Think

Your mind is where the battle is really taking place. Thoughts are past tense, meaning they're old. Thinking is present tense, meaning it's what you're doing right now. If you're not thinking about negative things right now, there's a good chance you won't do negative things later. Thoughts, become words, become actions, become you.

Truthfully, I have a whole board of directors that oversee my thinking. When I'm thinking something, I run it by one of them. However, they're not always going to be there. Eventually, I had to learn to think for myself. My best life coach, Mr. Henry Shelton, taught me the greatest lesson. Here is what he told me:

- Acknowledge your thoughts
    - Notice what and how you think.
    - Observe what you think about on a regular basis.
    - Realize they're just thoughts...that doesn't mean they are reality.
- Love or embrace your thoughts
    - Say to yourself, "It's okay that I had that thought. I'm human."
- Then change your thoughts
    - Make a conscious decision to think positively.

For example:
- If you think someone is ugly, find something that's beautiful in her or on her and focus on that.
- If someone gets on your nerves, think one good thing about that person and focus on that.
- Counter all negative thoughts with positive ones.
    - Don't say to yourself, "I'm dumb or stupid." Say to yourself "I'm getting wiser and smarter."
    - Don't say to yourself, "I'm broke and I'll never make it." Say to yourself, "Everything is going to be okay. I'm going through this for a reason."

The Vicious Cycle: A Key to Unlocking the Revolving Door

No matter what anyone thinks of you, what you think about yourself is MORE important. We all have flaws, and life is always going to come with challenges. People are always going to have something to say, so let them talk. It's very important to have a healthy self-image. Think and speak highly of yourself even when you don't see it. Speak things into being or existence. If you think it, you speak it, you see or visualize it, and you'll become it!

Before letting anything bother you OUTSIDE of yourself, find out why it's bothering you by asking yourself some questions.

For example:
- If you're mad, ask yourself
    - Why are you mad?
    - What are you really mad about?
    - Is it's worth your energy?
    - Do you really want to entertain this battle or can you let this go and be all right?"
- Substitute worried, afraid, or any other negative emotion for mad.

Pick and choose your battles wisely (this will reduce more stress than you know). If you don't have to battle with anyone else, then don't. Always try to find the part you played in the situation and use that as the reason you do not react but respond. This section of the Alcoholic Anonymous book worked wonders for me and taking this step.

> *"Our actor is self-centered—ego-centric, as people like to call it nowadays. He is like the retired business man who lolls in the Florida sunshine in the winter complaining of the sad state of the nation; the minister who sighs over the sins of the twentieth century; politicians and reformers who are sure all would be Utopia if the rest of the world would only behave; the outlaw safe cracker who thinks society has wronged him; and the alcoholic who has lost all and is locked*

up. Whatever our protestations, are not most of us concerned with ourselves, our resentments, or our-self-pity?

"Selfishness and self-centeredness! That is the root of our troubles. Driven by a hundred forms of fear, self-delusion, self-seeking, and self-pity, we step on the toes of our fellows and they retaliate. Sometimes they hurt us, seemingly without provocation, but we invariably find that at some time in the past we have made decisions based on self which later placed us in a position to be hurt.

"So our troubles are basically of our own making. They arise out of ourselves, and the alcoholic is an extreme example of self-will run riot, though he usually doesn't think so. Above everything, we must be rid of this selfishness. We must, or it kills us! God makes that possible. And there often seems no way of entirely getting rid of self without His aid. Many of us had moral and philosophical convictions galore, but we could not live up to them even though we would've like to. Neither could we reduce our self-centeredness much by wishing or trying on our own power. We had to have God's help."*

Taking responsibility for the part you played will help you and apologizing will disarm your opponent. Sometimes it'll make you mad, too. They'll agree with you like it was really all your fault, but you know better. It's not your fault, and that is not important. What you are doing has more to do with yourself and your peace of mind and less to do with them.

* Alcoholics Anonymous - Alcoholics Anonymous World Services, Inc. - 2009 - 4th Ed. - The Big Book Online - Alcoholics Ano... - ISBN: 1-893007-16-2

Step 2-Control Your Emotions

Emotions are like the steering wheel of the car. If you have the wrong passenger, driver, and/or destination, you will go in all the wrong directions. On the flip side of that coin is this: emotions are like the steering wheel of the car. If you have the RIGHT passenger, driver, and/or destination, you will go in all the RIGHT directions. Decisions made from an emotional standpoint are usually not very good ones. Things said when in an emotional state are usually harmful. You cannot take those words back. Calm down and think. Meditate if you must!

Check yourself by Step 1 before interacting with others or making decisions. Ask yourself...

- Should I talk to somebody who can calm me down before I say or do anything?
- What am I thinking right now?
- Do I love myself?
- What is a positive thing in this situation?
- How would I feel about myself if I end up doing something wrong?
- Why is this bothering me?
- Is this a battle I want to entertain?
- Is it worth my energy?
- How did I get in this situation in the first place?
- Where did I go wrong in this situation?

After asking yourself all of those things, now you have taken your power back and you can control your emotions. When you have a hold on your emotions, what do you do with them? To control means "to dominate or command". You must dominate and command your emotions! You are still going to feel them, and this doesn't take the pain or whatever you are feeling away. BUT, you must do your best to dominate or command them into a positive outlet. This transmutation or channeling is an alchemical process. Alchemy is the process of transmuting a common substance, usually of little value, into a substance of great value. What the positive outlet should be and how to figure it out leads us to the next step.

Step 3- Find a New Method of Stress Relief

As stated earlier, meditation works wonders. After meditating for the past four years, I can honestly say it's the reason that I am as successful today. Remaining grateful at all times IS THE KEY TO HAPPINESS. Meditation helps me to gain insight and take effective action.

Find something you love to do. Dr. Farrah Gray asks three questions on how to find your purpose in life in his book, *Get Real, Get Rich*. I suggest you read this book.

1. What would you do all day every day even if you never got paid for it?
2. What do you do better than most people?
3. How can you give back and be of service to society?

These three questions will show you your life's work and purpose. Your answers are very important. If you are having trouble answering them, go outdoors to a park or lake and sit quietly for a while. The answers will come to you. There are plenty of things you can do to reduce stress without picking up drugs and alcohol or committing a crime.

Remember everything you are grateful for. You may be incarcerated, but you're still alive. Thank God for each day in which you are awake. A gratitude list is a great way to remember all the reasons you should be happy. When we're grateful for all that we have, we open the door to receive the full abundance God has in store. Start with listing twenty things daily that you are grateful for, even if five of them are your five senses! It's important to acknowledge everything you are thankful for BEFORE asking God for more!

My last recommendation to reduce stress is to create a vision board to maintain your focus. Every year I create a vision board and find pictures, phrases, or draw images that are in alignment with the goals I have set for my life.

All you need is a poster board or large sheet of paper and some tape. Get pictures out of magazines, your own photos, or draw pictures that give you a visual illustration of what you aspire to accomplish, to have, or to become. When times are at their lowest, concentrate on that board! When you're tired and ready to give up, your vision board helps you remember why you started in the first place. Visualizing your vision board while meditating is also something you should do routinely.

It's very important to have a physical visual reminder of why you will overcome hardships and obstacles to escape the vicious cycle. A mental vision board is not enough. It should be a physical collage.

Sometimes all we need is a little motivation of our own to help us achieve goals. Like Zig Ziglar says, "Of course motivation is not permanent. But then, neither is bathing. It's something you should do on a regular basis."

Practical Exercises to Began Applying to Your Life

Do each exercise listed below, in order and as demonstrated in this book, every day for the next 30 days to began changing your life...

1. Keep a personal journal of your thoughts and emotions.
    a. Journaling can also include rapping, song writing, or poetry but write it down and try to make it positive. Remember... "Successful people find a way to get what they want and have what they want WITHOUT violating the rights of others."- Napoleon Hill, *Laws of Success*
    b. Every morning when you wake up, write a list of 20 things for which you are grateful and 20 things, in which you have no control.
        i. For example:
           I'm grateful for...
              God
              Good health

              My home
              My children
              My education
              Freedom, etc
           I'm powerless over...

       other people
       weather conditions
       traffic
       my parents, etc...

2. Meditate using one of the two techniques listed in this chapter for 5-10 minutes, preferably at the beginning AND end of the day.
3. Create a vision board for the entire year using the technique listed in this chapter, and memorize every detail of it by focusing on it for a few minutes a day
4. Read the excerpt from the AA book on page 48-49 of this book daily
5. Practice the steps also included in this chapter (Change Your Thinking, Control Your Emotions, Find a New Method of Stress Relief or Something You Love to Do)
   a. Use your journal to come up with answers to the questions about your thoughts and emotions, in order to began monitoring them regularly
6. Every night before you go to bed, reflect on your day. Write a couple of sentences or paragraphs about your thoughts, feelings, and actions of the day and what you could have done better.

    If you follow these steps and practice, practice, PRACTICE, you will begin to notice some changes, and after a period of time you will be on track to a life of success and enjoyment. Nothing comes overnight! These things take time and regular practice! Sometimes you will get it; sometimes you will not, but keep trying. Remember the story of the carrot, egg, and the coffee bean. Which one are you?

    In conclusion, my prayer is that this book provides the catalyst for your change. I hope it inspires you to reach for the stars. The sky is not the limit, because there are footprints on the moon, and the only limitations in life are the ones you set with your own mind.

    To your success!

About the Author

After overcoming the obstacles of adolescence, Crystal Victoria redefined her image by creating an opportunity for herself and the younger generation. While growing up in Denton, Texas, she endured many struggles for acceptance and endured a disturbing journey to satisfy the means. Although she was intelligent and had a college education, she had difficulty searching for a purpose and maintaining rewarding success.

At the age of 25, she found her calling and passion through motivation, business, and writing. Now today at the age of 28, she is the president and founder of Target Evolution, Inc., a motivational speaker, published author, and business developer who loves to read and learn. Her future plans consist of pursuing a doctorate's in business administration and business law, as well as continuing to support young entrepreneurs in the Dallas community and nationwide.

From the Streets to the Skies No Limits: Diary of a Boss Lady is the book about her life, revealing the strong woman behind the business, and how she became the change she wanted to see.

Have you or a family member felt like a victim of the revolving door of jails, prisons, and institutions? Are you searching for a way out? Or a way to help a loved one get out and stay out of the judicial system? YOU ARE NOT ALONE, but taking the first step to look and ask for help has lead you to this book, "The Vicious Cycle: A Key to Unlocking the Revolving Door". It will answer some of the questions you've probably always asked. How and why do people continue to live in and out of jail?

According to the Bureau of Justice Statistics there are currently 2.3 million people incarcerated in prisons and jails across America. Nationally, 97% of the offenders in jail today will be released and then return to the communities from which they came. Statistics show that 30% of adult offenders released from state prisons are re-arrested within the first six months of their release. Even worse, within three years of their release from prison this increases to 67%, or two out of three, ex-offenders returning to prison. Sadly, revocations are the fastest growing category of prison admissions. Parole violators now account for 35% of new prison admissions as compared to only 17% in 1980.

Every day thousands of people continue to make choices that lead them down a road of self-destruction and imprisonment. The good news is there is help and there is hope! In this book, you will learn:

- The mindset associated with repeat offenders
- How recidivism affects families
- What your family can do to help a loved one
- Community resources available in your area
- Practical tools to use to avoid trouble
- How to find a place to live ...AND
- How to become successful with a criminal background using my steps to success

A few years ago, I took action and today I use my personal testimony and strategies to help others whom have lost their way in this journey we call "life". Chin up! It's not over, in fact, this is a new beginning! A new life of peace and fulfillment awaits! Let's get started...

The Vicious Cycle: A Key to Unlocking the Revolving Door

The Vicious Cycle: A Key to Unlocking the Revolving Door

www.ingramcontent.com/pod-product-compliance
Lightning Source LLC
Chambersburg PA
CBHW071545080526
44588CB00011B/1806